pictureshowpress.net

"In Praise of Thick Thighs" first appeared in *A Teenager's Guide to Feminism* (Pear Shaped Press) and "Mata Hari Dances" was previously published in *Circus Noir* (Yak Press, 2019).

Cover: ivanastar, istockphoto.com
Cover font: Calligraffiti[1]

FIRST EDITION

ISBN-13: 978-1-7341702-5-2

The Undulating Line

Writing Poetry through Belly Dance

EDITORS

Suzanne Allen

Shannon Phillips

Aruni Wijesinghe

Picture Show Press

Contents

Introduction

When I was 15 years old (an impressionable age!), I first saw the music video for a popular U2 song, "Mysterious Ways." Well, the music video featured a belly dancer, and I was, effectively, hooked. Ten years later, I took a semester of belly dance, and my love for Middle Eastern music took hold.

Since then, I have read a lot about cultural appropriation, and what I can say is that I am still listening and learning. Even the term "belly dance" has its issues. A better name for it is *raqs sharqee*, but for multiple reasons — some technical, some beyond — I've chosen to go with "belly dance." For one, once you learn how to write in a different alphabet, transliterated terms can often become unsatisfactory to you.

I studied Arabic formally for two years, mostly because I love language and also because I wanted to enhance my ability to write poetry. The phrase "Arabic poetry" might even be redundant because, to many, the language itself is poetic, and poetry is highly valued in Arabic culture. (Of course, I realize belly dance is not only practiced by Arabic-speaking peoples.)

First and foremost, this is an experimental book of poetry, and as such, the focus is on poetry. It goes without saying that language has many uses, but at its base, language is about communicating, about expressing oneself. And even though it may not seem like it to some, poetry is ultimately about expressing oneself as well, in an attempt to connect with another (sometimes that "other" may even be yourself). Dance embodies the same goal, but with the added benefit of celebration.

This book is a celebration of that impulse, that desire to express, move, and connect.

— *Shannon, editor*

"Poems are a form of music, and language just happens to be our instrument — language and breath."
~ Terrance Hayes

"As a writer, even as a child, long before what I wrote began to be published, I developed a sense that meaning itself was resident in the rhythms of words and sentences and paragraphs..."
~ Joan Didion

"Celebrate!": Body Image, Belly Dance, and the Ode

"When you dance, you can enjoy the luxury of being you."
~ Paulo Coelho

"We dance to seduce ourselves. To fall in love with ourselves. When we dance with another, we manifest the very thing we love about ourselves so that they may see it and love us too."
~ Kamand Kojouri

-1-

Many people battle with self-image on a daily basis, and it is not uncommon to have a sense of dissatisfaction about one's body. Part of the beauty of belly dance is the opportunity to celebrate the body as it exists, whole and complete, and the permission to set down the need to criticize perceived imperfections. Dance is a time to cast off inhibitions and self-criticism and live in the moment.

THE ODE

An ode is a type of formal lyric poem that celebrates anything from a person to an idea. There is more than one type; Pindaric odes are publicly recited poems that commemorate an athletic victory, whereas Horatian odes are more meditative. In the past, musicians and dancers were included in the performance of a Pindaric ode.

Here we want to write more in the English Romantic style because we will be praising a body part. This style often concludes with a revelation of some kind. Expressing intense emotion is also encouraged.

If you prefer to work within a frame, consider writing in the structure of a Sapphic ode, using quatrains, which contain three 11-syllable lines, and a final line of five syllables. Typically, Sapphic odes do not rhyme.

OBJECTIVE

- Write an ode to a body part that you love; or
- Write an ode celebrating a body part that you don't love.

Check out the example odes on the following pages.

RECOMMENDED READING

"homage to my hips" by Lucille Clifton
"Ode to Fat" by Ellen Bass

The curves of her

stop me every time,
encircled in a spell,
my feet refuse to move an inch.

Her stomach peeks through
the gap between her blouse and skirt,
enticing me with its skin,
paler than the rest.

I stare.
I shouldn't, but I am captured.

Her hands try to hide it,
tugging her shirt down
to cover the beautiful rolls of flesh.

I want to slap that hand away.

I want to see her — all of her,
pale flesh rolls that curve
and spread to wide hips.

A belly button plays peek-a-boo,
tempting, teasing for the world to see.

I shake my head out of the trance I am in,
take one last glance in the mirror
and leave.

— *Kitty Moffett*

In Praise of Thick Thighs

She rubs her thighs together,
bow against bow, quivering
the strings of a primal call
Thick thighs are a portal
to an inner universe

rounded thighs rubbed
with sandalwood paste
ample like feast days,
tabletop enough to hold
pitchers of yogurt, bowls of butter

sacred thighs, the pillars
of the temple where we come
to worship, prostrate ourselves
on the altar of plenty,
gorge ourselves on flesh
and enlightenment

thick thighs, two columns uphold
the pelvic bowl where we come
to burn offerings of animal fat and incense
phalanx of thick-thigh'd girls adorns
the temple frieze, provokes
cellulite-fueled paroxysms of ecstasy

Devotees of the Cult of Thick
sway and faint, enraptured
by the applause of thick thighs
running up the temple stairs

stilled thighs buttress the sanctuary walls
priestess swoons over the fumes,
predicting the razing of cities,
the fall of empires

fevered thighs vibrate
with the primordial pulse
friction kindles fire, catches the tinder
of a nation's drowsing amygdala

Thick thighs are made to withstand
the long climb uphill
to unseat emperors,
topple rawboned deities.

— *Aruni Wijesinghe*

Exquisite Corpse

"I love how rabbis so often say, 'The teacher of my teacher says...' I love that genealogy, that reminder of kinship, care."
                              ~ Claire Schwartz, Tweet, 6 March 2019

~2~

"Write one line, fold the paper over and pass it on."

That was how Vivienne Vermes introduced me to the game years before I learned its name or where it had come from, and yet there we were, in Paris on a rainy spring evening near Montparnasse. It seemed implausible enough, so we sipped and sighed, rubbed our heads, fumbled with the folding and nibbled if we finished before the timer, sometimes scribbling desperately past it. We were eight around her dining room table.

Part salon and part séance, the soirée was lit with candles and watered with wine, paced by short stretches of writing and taking turns reading and remarking around the long dining table, and olives, cheese, and mini blinis with crème fraiche and capers. When the myriad folds were smoothed and the handwriting decoded, we found the "poems" were resonances... among... what? Strangers, mostly, to me anyway. Expats, all, motley and strangely familiar, and our collected absurdities written between the fold lines were strangely cohesive, too, and absolutely and perfectly exquisite.

In those months before I left Paris and for a couple of years after that, I attributed the magic of those sublime bits of sense in nonsense to *her*, to Vivienne and the irreplicable coincidences of an enchanted evening *chez elle*.

Eventually I learned that the "game" is called Exquisite Corpse, and that it was 'invented' by the French Surrealists. In *The Poet's Companion*, Kim Addonizio and Dorianne Laux include it as one of their suggested writing ideas in the chapter, "Stop Making Sense: Dreams and Experiments." They list four essential elements of surrealist poetics: "surprise, juxtaposition, openness, and movement." See? This explains why, when Shannon got her belly dancer tattoo and started dreaming of "The Undulating Line," my mind went straight to it. It makes perfect sense now, my whole long story with it.

Most special about this particular take on the now old favorite of mine is that it's the first time the group has been all women, an ambiance further enhanced by the seed words we wrote at the bottom of each page to filter the elements of belly dance into the more general things plaguing our minds at the same time. This is a layer I've used with great effect in ESL classes, by the way. It's perfect for practicing various aspects of grammar and vocabulary, but here, in this context, it allowed us to explore aspects of the dance by steering us ever into the words of it as we stitched out lines.

Now, after years of bending this "game" to my purposes and whims, I see it as a happening, performative in its process and full of possibilities for extension of the performance. It can also be played between visual artists, and while the players matter immensely, what matters more is that this game is at once in the moment AND completely beyond it, forever inextricable from the collective energy, time and place that bore it and leading to a documented subconsciousness of the fleeting moment.

Take a look at our results. These lines were written on a Sunday afternoon in an otherwise empty dance studio in a small shopping center in Brea, California after forty-five minutes of shake and shimmy in front of the mirrors with a bunch of women who mostly hadn't met before. I no longer even remember which lines are "mine." Or were. Or never were. And in a way, they're all mine, ours. All of ours.

STEPS

There are many ways to approach creating an Exquisite Corpse.

For our workshop, we each chose a word or two and scrawled it at the bottom of our own paper, leaving it visible. Then we wrote our first line at the top of the page and folded it back so it couldn't be read before passing our paper to the person on our left, where they could then add the next line. Each participant repeated this action until everyone's pages had cycled through. Finally, once our papers were returned to us, we added one last line before unfurling our collective poem.

A tulip is a glittering coquette

Have you ever tried to play a violin?
Every mistake happens too close to your face.
The curve of the violin reminds me of her, strings
begging to be plucked, hard seat of its heart.
The curve of her body is like mine, but different.
A harmony searching with all its might, years
of plucking strings — so many ways to play that song,
or write a love letter. The string is bowed, then plucked,
then breaks into song. A violin might love.

My body is not a four-cornered room

I always fall for the feminine curve
Carve this space for you, claiming the melody
The shimmy of your shoulders is an invitation.
The fine brush strokes
The brushstrokes of her arm
Brush my hair. Carve the shape of a woman.
Brush your hair back from your eyes.
The feminine is fierce — do not tread.
My body is the whole damn house.

Contributors:

Suzanne Allen
Christina Brown
Sallie Cordova Gallagher
Kelly Heinlein
Kitty Moffett
Heather Pease
Shannon Phillips
Aruni Wijesinghe
Nancy Lynée Woo

"What can't you get away from?" Exploring the Ghazal

"My library is an archive of longings."
~ Susan Sontag

"We look at the world once, in childhood. The rest is memory."
~ Louise Glück

"still laughing with two old
best friends, as if time doesn't pass

but only flips over and over
itself like a coin in the cover

of cupped hands."
~ Taylor Byas, "Growing Pains"

~3~

Not only does belly dance come from the same region as the ghazal, both artistic forms rely on refrain as a device. Dance contains refrains as part of the pattern (with variation) and many languages of the Middle East and Western Asia use a recursive style that includes refrain and a rephrasing of the same concept in different words.

Typically, the ghazal is a love poem used to express longing. The form was also used to express a metaphysical love or a desire for spiritual completeness.

In your writing, what is it that you can't get away from?

I can't get away from my 15-year-old self (sometimes it's my 25-year-old self). Or a lot of times, it's someone I've desired.

> *You share a kiss with someone, and one month, one year, ten years later, you slam your car door and happen to look up at the moon and that person's breath is back on your skin.*

Unrequited, longing.

Memory is not linear; we try to contain it, to anchor it — *that's when I was attending classes at that school downtown* or *there was that time I was waiting tables* — but why do we do this? Does memory really know of a timeline? There is no beginning, no middle, no end. Western thought teaches us to organize our thinking this way, but there are other ways.

With the ghazal, repeat the thing you need to say; repeat what is important. Say it with different words, in different ways.

- A ghazal contains anywhere between five and fifteen couplets.
- Each couplet is grammatically complete and can stand on its own, but the couplets are linked by theme and by rhyme scheme.
- Each couplet carries the same end-word, e.g. *hips*.
- Each couplet contains a rhyming word that comes before the end-word, e.g. "blue hips" and "glue hips."
- The rhyming word and the end-word appear twice in the first couplet.
- Try to keep your couplets at approximately the same length.
- A name (can be a diminutive), usually that of the poet, appears in the final couplet.

TIPS

- When generating work, remember that gibberish is perfectly okay, even encouraged. Ghazals were performed. Play with sounds. Have at it. Have fun.
- If you can't think of anything to write, write down all the names you've ever been called.
- Writing 101: Concrete is always better. In my sophomore year of high school, my teacher asked us to complete the sentence, *Love is...* and I wrote something Latinate and

platitudinal. I had to resubmit the assignment. I passed with "Love is the smell of bacon and box-mix blueberry muffins on a Saturday morning."

- Always, always — if something you're writing is working, feel free to modify the "rules" of the form and/or drop them altogether.

Check out the example ghazal on the following page (the couplet form was overridden for formatting reasons).

RECOMMENDED READING

"Hip-Hop Ghazal" by Patricia Smith

Mata Hari Dances

Everything is an illusion.
— Mata Hari, femme fatale

Young girl thin, sheds her skin, embraces sin in both arms. Like
    a snake,
trades school for cool jewels, new tools, her arms like a snake.

Black curls, skirts whirl, veils unfurl, she writhes lithe. Blue
smoke from the pipe, woman archetype, she charms like a snake.

Olive skin whispers gin in diplomat's ears, and secrets spill tears
easy down officers' throats. She gloats, disarms like a snake.

She purrs in furs, false demure, allegiance blurs. Follow the money,
keep moving, honey. Wraps her bones around stones, she
    warms like a snake.

Military indiscretion, forced confession, French obsession.
Betrayal complete, ground beneath her feet drops the beat,
    rattles warning, alarms like a snake.

Java princess or mourning mother, courtesan or jilted lover —
history's pawn, Eye of the Dawn, reinvents events against the
    scorn that harms like a snake.

Easy scapegoat, she wraps her coat around her throat. Spy caught
in the spotlight, she kisses the firing squad goodnight.
    Gendarmes fire; she falls like a snake.

Margaretha Zelle casts her spell, casts off the final veil. All's fair
    in dance
and war. Bejeweled in lore, history's whore, elusive as the arms
    of a snake.

— *Aruni Wijesinghe*

Erasure Poetry:
Carving a Space for Yourself

-4-

We've all been made fun of, called names, but have you ever had your face get hot after being called a "bitch" or a "slut"?

How many of you now dance without shame in front of the mirror to "WAP," a song by rap artists Cardi B and Megan Thee Stallion?

That's right! Me, me, me!!

That is exactly how you take back words and make them your own.

Taking back words is not a new idea. In 1998, Inga Muscio wrote *Cunt*, a book that delves into the history of the word and makes a case for "reclaiming" it from its negative connotations. And before that, there was *The Vagina Monologues*, a play written by Eve Ensler.

Belly dance has been sexualized for some time now, although its origins are rooted in fertility and childbirth ritual. I will never forget when a friend of mine, who is from Lebanon, told me that when she was a child, she told her mother that she wanted to be a dancer and her mother told her to never say that to anyone ever again.

Even though it is a dance that is ideally supposed to be performed for women by women, it does have a tawdry reputation, first and foremost, since many believe its purpose is to entertain men. Naturally, everyone has a choice in who to dance for — whether it be for themselves or for others — and this is exactly as it should be. And for those who are inspired, you can always "take back" the dance from the male gaze.

If you refuse to exist solely in the boxes that the patriarchy has set out for you — wife, mother, daughter, sister, to name a few — in belly dance, you would literally carve out your own space with gestures and dance movements, refusing to make yourself smaller.

In poetry, you can also thwart the status quo by writing in the erasure "form" (or really, in any form talked about in this book). It may seem like a small gesture, but small steps, as anyone can tell you, is how anything happens. Make no mistake — the English language is a tool that reinforces the dominant power structure, but we all have to use it so make it do what you want it to.

According to the Academy of American Poets, "Erasure poetry may be used [...] as a means of confrontation, a challenge to a pre-existing text." The poet Isobel O'Hare does this in *all this can be yours*, her collection of erasure poems created from #metoo apologies. When writing an erasure poem, a poet gets to choose the words that they want to use in order to tell the story that they want to tell.

To write an erasure poem, choose a text (Take a crack at the canon!) and erase, black out, or somehow cover up most of the source text, leaving only those words that express what you have to say.

On the following pages, check out the two visual versions of Aruni Wijesinghe's "Her Tale Begins," which she carved out of the prologue[2] to *A Thousand and One Nights*.

Her Tale Begins

sister, I want your help
as a last favour —

your company
the last night I am alive

wake me before the dawn
and speak, I beg you

one of your charming stories
shall deliver the people

the hour arrived:
bade her raise her veil,
her eyes full

a sister
tenderly grant me

before the sun rises,
one of your charming stories

pleasure of hearing you
answer, sister

As my sister asks,
said she.

So, Scheherazade began.

sister; I want your help

as a last favour
last night I am alive.
the dawn, and speak

one of your charming stories   shall

deliver the people

your company   the
wake me   before
I beg you

the   hour arrived

bade her raise her veil

a sister

Grant me

her eyes full

tenderly

before the sun rises, one of your charming stories.

pleasure of hearing you."

answer   sister,
as my sister asks?" said she.

So Scheherazade began.

31

Figure 8: Concrete Poetry

In life, as in art, the beautiful moves in curves.
~ Edward G. Bulwer-Lytton

~5~

Prologue

5:30 am.

I heard my son calling me. Another bad dream?

At least, I thought I'd heard him calling me.

Over four fans strategically placed throughout our one-bedroom apartment, I thought I'd heard my son calling me. It had been hot for several days straight.

When I went to check on him, he turned out to be sound asleep. That smooth, beautiful non-look look of surrender.

Afterward, I lay down and tried to fall back asleep, but I couldn't. A poem, out of nowhere, came tumbling out of my mind's own night sky. Lines like light.

I was tired. I had been too busy editing other people's stuff. Repeat after me: I have been too busy [fill in the blank] other people's stuff. (See: capitalism. Insert: sigh, weary and wary.)

I, mother/daughter/sister/partner (circle any and all that apply), have been too busy to work on my own stuff.

And so, without my realizing, this chapter and its companion "essay" went on the back burner of my brain, and what does my brain do (maybe yours does this, too) when I sleep? It solves problems; it gave me this solution. It gave me a poem.

I had to get up.

*   *   *

Perhaps a poem can be the solution.

In *A Primer for Poets and Readers of Poetry*, Gregory Orr talks about the "ordering power" or "ordering principles" of poetry, as well as its "expressive structure." He goes on to say that applying poetry's organizing principles can help us process something we're going through.

What might be some of those "ordering principles"? Maybe a title; the stanza, line breaks. Music. Grammar.

To add even more "organization" or "structure," try writing a poem in the shape of an object, or what is known as "concrete" poetry. Essentially, concrete poetry is a combination of visual and literary art[3].

Fawzia, the author of the book *Grandmother's Secrets*, writes that her grandmother used the Arabic alphabet to teach her about belly dance. Her grandmother instructed her to stand like the alif

ﺍ, and move her hips in the shape of the baa ﺏ, taa ﺕ, and thaa ﺙ.

> *"Dancing is creating a sculpture that is visible only for a moment."*
>
> ~ *Erol Ozan*

What is the "expressive structure" of belly dance? Your camels, your shimmies, your snake arms, your lifts, your drops.

In belly dance, the figure 8 is one of the key shapes you make with your body. Over and over. Undulate. Pulse. Hips. Vertical. Horizontal. Forward. Backward.

In dance, we make shapes.

How do we do this in writing? Or more specifically, how do we do it in this book?

With a poem that twists. That makes a figure 8. This poem can be handwritten — it can go up diagonally, or down diagonally, and over, and under. It can round at the top. And curve at the bottom. It can be word art. Word search. Words or letters can be stacked vertically, to be read from the bottom up or the top down. Or even tiered in a diagonal pattern. Up, down. Down, up. It can slope left, or it can slope right.

As with the erasure poem, think of it as "carving space."

Check out "untitled" by Shannon Phillips on the following page.

```
          She says,
   My            hips
  like           to eat.
  Eat            and
  pray,          she
  says.          Pray
  to my          hips.
 Tell me a       fortune.
 She says,       I have
 daughters.      I have no
 daughters,      daughters
  to camp        on the
      embankment of my
        hips, daughters
  to rise        on the
 sunset of       my hips.
 Scorching       sculptural
 horizon of      my hips.
 She says,       My stretch
 marks are       diamond
 lassos          embracing
 my hips.        My hips
  like to        eat love
  made by        warm
  palms.         The sun
 shines on       my hips.
  Sunshine       on my
    hips. And the moon, she says.
    How could I forget about the moon.
```

"Mirror, mirror": The Palindrome

"Poets are word fetishists, among other things, and their grounding belief is that language is humankind's greatest technology, inexhaustible, endlessly adaptable, a mirror of a poet's own time and, hopefully, of the endless unfolding of all time."

~ Craig Morgan Teicher, "We Begin In Gladness"

~6~

If you're adept at taking selfies for your social media profiles, you probably know which "side" is your "good side." The same goes for a dancer. A belly dancer may make a perfect camel with their dominant side, but they will still practice a move on both "sides" because what one hip (or shoulder or wrist) does, the other must repeat in kind.

In this way, body parts mirror or reflect their opposite. Likewise, poetry can be a powerful way to reflect.

> *"Why poetry?*
> *Because I can move in poetry in ways that I cannot otherwise."*
> *~ Rosebud Ben-Oni, Tweet, 20 May 2019*

Like the figure 8, the palindrome never ends. It simply rolls or loops back onto itself. And like the ghazal — and much like memory — the palindrome has no discernible beginning, middle, and end; as such, it is not linear.

HOW TO WRITE YOUR OWN

Choose your words carefully because you will be using them in the first half and repeating them in reverse for the second. In the "middle," you will need a "bridge" word to connect the two halves.

Check out the sample poem, *Listen*, on the following page.

And remember, if something you're writing is working, and the rules of a form are getting in your way, change the rules or even scrap them. Writing the poem is more important.

RECOMMENDED READING

There is another type of palindrome or "mirror" poem that can be read from top to bottom and bottom to top.

"10-year-old pens a powerful palindrome about having dyslexia" (*twitter.com/i/event*, 27 Feb 2019).

"The True Meaning Behind This Poem Will Make Your Heart Soar" (Alcántara, Ann-Marie, *popsugar.com*, 26 Feb 2016).

Listen

Her hips speak *magic*. Music
stirs. Arms snake. An eight sways.
Her hands carve
an alphabet
is carved in her hands.
Eight swaying snakes. Arms stir
music. *Magic*, says her hips.

— *Shannon Phillips*

Taqsim, Ekphrasis, and "The Arabic"

~7~

If you've enjoyed this book so far, and you like experimenting, read on for some more poem-generating ideas that work in the themes we've been discussing.

TAQSIM

A taqsim is an improvised piece of music that is common in Middle Eastern music, and it helps to know your stuff when dancing taqsim. How does this translate to poetry? Improvisation, spontaneity, and playfulness are all qualities of belly dance. This book has been organized around forms (though no one ever needs permission to deviate from them!), but a taqsim might be the equivalent to free verse or freestyle poetry. In dance, all you need are some moves and once you've got them, you can get out there and have some fun. Writing a poem can be the same. Keeping in mind these values — improvisation, spontaneity, playfulness — substitute "moves" for techniques — or even vocabulary or images — and get out there and go shake it on the page!

Need a word bank? There are plenty of words in this book. I recommend revisiting the section on Exquisite Corpse or the ghazal. Lots of gorgeous inspiration for your taqsim there.

EKPHRASIS

An ekphrastic poem is written in conversation with a specific work of art. The more classic take is one of a poem vividly describing a scene, but it can also be an opportunity to examine your own lens, your way of looking at things. As with the erasure poem, you can reframe a subject the way you want to see it — have your say, your voice, your choice — look through different eyes, prize and prioritize a different "gaze" (male or female, for example, and what does that mean? Write toward an answer, your answer).

To honor the vibe in this book, consider attempting an ekphrastic poem about the Arabesque[4] pattern on display at the end of this chapter.

"THE ARABIC"

If the moments in this book that talk about challenging the patriarchal status quo spoke to you or you've been curious about or are into translation, then you may want to consider trying out a poetic form created by Marwa Helal called "The Arabic." The poem is meant to be read from right to left and you can stop there, but there are a few other elements. The form dictates that the poem contain:

- an Arabic letter
- an Arabic numeral
- an Arabic footnote

Also, unlike the palindrome, this poem should not make any sense when read from left to right, only from right to left, like the Arabic language. This last requirement is fueled by Helal's rejection of standards imposed by anglophone colonizers.

REQUIRED READING

"POEM TO BE READ FROM RIGHT TO LEFT" by Marwa Helal can be found in *Winter Tangerine*.

Endnotes

1. "Calligraffitti by Open Window owes its credit to mom and all her years of Calligraphic experience. This impromptu rendering of her calligraphic alphabet captures her years or formal practice blended with a rare encounter with the mood altering music of Santana" (*fonts.google.com*).

2. "People focus on the dynamic between Scherezade and the sultan, but the first tale is told at the request of Scherezade's sister. In essence, the narrative impetus is the request of a woman. And a woman is responsible for hatching the plan that saves her sister." ~ Aruni Wijesinghe

3. Dubai's emir, Sheikh Muhammad, may even eventually take the concrete poem to a level beyond if his vision of a manmade coastline in the shape of a poem he wrote is one day realized. (Whether or not it should be is a topic for another essay.)

4. Image licensed under Creative Commons CC0 1.0 Universal Public Domain Dedication and made available by Jebulon, *commons.wikimedia.org*, 14 August 2012 ("Detail arabesque Alhambra Granada Spain.jpg").

Bibliography

"A Brief Guide to Concrete Poetry." *poets.org*

Addonizio, Kim, and Dorianne Laux. *The Poet's Companion: A Guide to the Pleasures of Writing Poetry*. New York, W.W. Norton & Company, 1997.

Al-Rawi, R. B. *Grandmother's Secrets: The Ancient Rituals and Healing Power of Belly Dancing*. Northampton, MA: Interlink Publishing Group, 2000.

Barokka, Khairani. "The Case Against Italicizing 'Foreign' Words." *Catapult Magazine*. 11 Feb 2020. catapult.co

Berman, Judy. "Reclaiming the C Word ... again." *salon.com*, 1 Sept 2009.

Brabant, M. "Egyptian belly dance 'in crisis.'" *BBC News*, 30 March 2005. news.bbc.co.uk

Brewer, Robert Lee. "Poetic Form: Palindrome poetry (or mirror poem)." *Writer's Digest*, 18 Nov 2010.

Chen, Joyce. "The Politics of Gatekeeping: On Reconsidering the Ethics of Blind Submissions." *Poets & Writers*. 7 Oct 2020.

"Concrete poetry." *poetryfoundation.org*

"Egyptian Belly Dancers." *National Geographic*, 31 Jan 2011. youtube.com

"Ekphrasis." *poetryfoundation.org*

"Ekphrasis: Poetry Confronting Art." *poets.org*, 31 Jan 2005.

"Erasure." *poets.org*.

Gardner, F. "Belly Dancing Goes Global." *BBC News*, 6 June 2001. news.bbc.co.uk

"Ghazal." *poetryfoundation.org*

"Ghazal." *poets.org*

Goff, Nichole. "Erasure, Grief, and the Underworld - an Interview with Isobel O'Hare." *1508 [A Blog Where Poetry Lives]*, 6 Aug 2018. poetry.arizona.edu

Gomaa-Moulds, Lina. "5 Writing Trouble Spots for ESL Students of Arabic." 1 Nov 2010. pdxscholar.library.pdx.edu

Gordon, J. "DANCE; Moving With the Spirit Of Salome." *The New York Times*, 21 May 2006. query.nytimes.com

Haffner, Erin, and Donna Hilbert. "Poetry and the Body." Golden West College (workshop). 2 Feb 2019.

Higgins, Charlotte. "The Age of Patriarchy: How an Unfashionable Idea Became a Rallying Cry for Feminism Today." *The Guardian*, 22 June 2018.

Jarrar, Randa. "Why I can't stand white belly dancers." *salon.com*, 5 March 2014.

---. "I still can't stand white belly dancers." *salon.com*, 19 March 2014.

Jennings, Ken. "The Real Story Behind Dubai's Palm Islands." *Condé Nast Traveler*, 23 Nov 2015. cntraveler.com

Jorgensen, Jeana. "Cultural Appropriation Vs. Borrowing in Belly Dance (Part 1)." *jeanajorgensen.com*, 13 March 2014.

Keyes, Abigail. "Why I'm Glad Belly Dance in the U.S. is Declining." *akeyesdance.com*, 28 June 2017.

Kitta, Andrea. "Response to 'Why I Can't Stand White Bellydancers'." American Folklore Society, 7 April 2014. afsnet.org

Knapp, Michaelsun. "Let the Music Take Control: Building Lyricism into Your Poem's Bones, Or: Cheating at Lyricism." *Culturama Community*. 9 Nov 2020.

Knell, Y. "Enduring Allure of Egyptian Belly Dance." *BBC News*, 18 July 2009. news.bbc.co.uk

Lang, Andrew. "Project Gutenberg's The Arabian Nights Entertainments." *gutenberg.org*, 9 June 2008.

"Ode." *poetryfoundation.org*

"Ode." *poets.org*

Orr, Gregory. *A Primer for Poets and Readers of Poetry*. New York, W.W. Norton & Company, 2018.

"Palindrome." *poetryfoundation.org*

Rufo, John. "'No Were There But': Marwa Helal's 'Poem to Be Read From Right to Left'." *Ploughshares*, 17 Nov 2016. blog.pshares.org

Sernaker, Emily. "The Ms. Q&A: How Poet Marwa Helal Uses Poetry as Preservation." *Ms.*, 8 Jan 2018. msmagazine.com

Schmidt, Samantha. "Why the c-word is so taboo, and why some women want to reclaim it." *Washington Post*, 1 June 2018.

"Suzanne Talhouk at TEDxBeirut 2012." *TEDx Talks*, 17 Dec 2012, youtube.com

"VOICES OF BETTERING AMERICAN POETRY VOLUME 3 — NOOR IBN NAJAM." *vidaweb.org*, 19 Feb 2019.

Well, Tara. "Taking Back the Male Gaze." *Psychology Today*, 6 Nov 2017.

Wetzler, Cynthia M. "For the Elderly, the Benefits of Belly Dance." *The New York Times*, 24 August 1997. nytimes.com

Acknowledgments

I need to say thank you to Brian Harman for listening to me spin while I was attempting to synthesize all of these ideas, and also for taking the lead on caring for our baby so I could free up the space to finish this project.

— *Shannon, editor*

About the Editors

Suzanne Allen is a former interior designer turned poet and writing instructor. She holds an MFA in Poetry from CSULB and has two chapbooks: *verisimilitude* from corrupt press, and *Little Threats* from Picture Show Press. To pay the bills, she teaches writing at Golden West College.

One February long ago in Paris, while completing her minor in French, she stumbled upon The Other Writers Group, which met each Sunday evening in the upstairs library at Shakespeare & Company, a semi-transient group of Anglophone writers that gave her a place to come back to after completing her MFA. She eventually became a guest facilitator there and also served as the Creative Writing Program Director for WICE, a non-profit cultural education organization for Anglophones, where she planned the courses and facilitated WICE Writers, a weekly drop-in workshop for members and other writers interested in joining. Since her mid-life retirement ended, she and her Shih Tzu, Filou, have moved back to Long Beach, but she holds on tight to that magic city as a long-distance coeditor for *The Bastille, the literary magazine of Spoken Word Paris* — an extension of The Other Writers Group — which still happens every Monday night at the Chat Noir.

Her poems have been published in print and online journals such as *Nerve Cowboy*, *Pearl*, *Spillway*, and *Tears in the Fence*, with awards from *California Quarterly*, *Cider Press Review*, and *Writing in a Woman's Voice*.

Shannon Phillips took a semester of belly dance at Orange Coast College over 15 years ago, but she has never stopped loving it or Middle Eastern music. In 2015, she started teaching ESL and through teaching, she met many students from Saudi Arabia and their camaraderie not only reignited that initial spark but spurred her into learning Arabic. In 2017, she earned an Associate of Arts degree in Arabic and embraced the full-fledged language nerd within.

Before that, Shannon earned her MFA in creative writing from California State University, Long Beach. Her poem, "Plum" placed second in Beyond Baroque's First Annual Poetry Contest. More recently, she received the 28th Moon prize from *Writing In A Woman's Voice*. In 2011, she started Carnival, an online literary magazine, which she eventually transitioned into Picture Show Press. She is also the co-founder of the annual Mother's Day poetry reading at Gatsby Books and has co-hosted that reading since 2012. She has published two chapbooks: *My Favorite Mistake* (Arroyo Seco Press) and *Body Parts* (dancing girl press).

Aruni Wijesinghe has worked as a project manager for Affinis Labs, a substitute ESL teacher, occasional sous chef and erstwhile dance instructor. She holds degrees in English literature, dance, and TESOL. Her work has been published by *Angels Flight — Literary West*, Moon Tide Press, Picture Show Press, Arroyo Seco Press, Tebot Bach (in the *Spillway* anthology), *Dryland Literary Journal* and elsewhere. Aruni also has two solo collections of poetry forthcoming in 2021 with Moon Tide Press and Silver Star Labs.

In the summer of 1993, Aruni attended her first belly dance class with her college roommate and it was love at first shimmy. She began taking classes at the Blanca Luz Academy of Dance under Sandra Luna and performed with the troupe, Jewels of Fire, for a number of years. As her interest in dance grew, Aruni continued to study Middle Eastern and other dance forms including ballet, jazz, modern, tap, Afro-Haitian, Polynesian, and flamenco, eventually earning an AA in dance from Cypress College. She focused her efforts mainly in perfecting her technique in Middle Eastern dance and has studied with many well-known artists, most notably the world-famous Angelika Nemeth; Aruni went on to be a dancer in the Angelika Nemeth Dance Ensemble for many years. She has performed and taught around Southern California and continues to seek out more opportunities to explore different dance and art forms.

When she is not furiously scribbling or twirling around her living room, Aruni lives a quiet life in Orange County with her husband Jeff and their cats, Jack and Josie.

Notes

www.ingramcontent.com/pod-product-compliance
Lightning Source LLC
Chambersburg PA
CBHW021142020426
42331CB00005B/866